How Energy Changed the World

Stephanie Feldstein

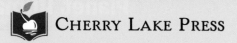

CHERRY LAKE PRESS

Published in the United States of America by Cherry Lake Publishing Group
Ann Arbor, Michigan
www.cherrylakepublishing.com

Reading Adviser: Beth Walker Gambro, MS, Ed., Reading Consultant, Yorkville, IL

Photo Credits: © Matthew Troke/Shutterstock, cover; © MarkVanDykePhotography/Shutterstock, 4; © Darren J. Bradley/Shutterstock, 6; © AorusVisuals/Shutterstock, 9; © small smiles/Shutterstock, 10; © Alex Tihonovs/Shutterstock, 11; From an article by Jack Harris, New Scientist (1982). The photo was taken between 1882-1886, whilst the Holborn Viaduct power station was running., Public domain, via Wikimedia Commons, 12; Bain News Service, publisher, Public domain, via Wikimedia Commons, 13; © Smile Fight/Shutterstock, 14; © Joseph Sohm/Shutterstock, 15; Frank J. Aleksandrowicz, National Archives, DOCUMERICA: The Environmental Protection Agency's Program to Photographically Document Subjects of Environmental Concern, 16; LeRoy Woodson, National Archives, DOCUMERICA: The Environmental Protection Agency's Program to Photographically Document Subjects of Environmental Concern, 17; © Shawn Talbot/Shutterstock, 19; © Sobrevolando Patagonia/Shutterstock, 20; © FenrisWolf/Shutterstock, 21; © Piotr Krzeslak/Shutterstock, 22; © VisualProduction/Shutterstock, 25; © Gary Perkin/Shutterstock, 26; © Diyana Dimitrova/Shutterstock, 27; © Gorodenkoff/Shutterstock, 28; © oneinchpunch/Shutterstock, 29; © Gerry Dincher from Hope Mills, NC, CC BY-SA 2.0 <https://creativecommons.org/licenses/by-sa/2.0>, via Wikimedia Commons, 30

Cherry Lake Press is an imprint of Cherry Lake Publishing Group.

Library of Congress Cataloging-in-Publication Data

Names: Feldstein, Stephanie, author.
Title: How energy changed the world / Written by Stephanie Feldstein.
Description: Ann Arbor, Michigan : Cherry Lake Publishing, 2024. | Series: Planet human | Audience: Grades 4-6 |
    Summary: "The energy industry has profoundly impacted our world. The Planet Human series breaks down the
    human impact on the environment over time and around the globe. Each title presents important high-interest
    natural science nonfiction content with global relevance"— Provided by publisher.
Identifiers: LCCN 2023035077 | ISBN 9781668939062 (paperback) | ISBN 9781668938027 (hardcover) |
    ISBN 9781668940402 (ebook) | ISBN 9781668941751 (pdf)
Subjects: LCSH: Energy industries—Juvenile literature. | Ecology—Juvenile literature.
Classification: LCC HD9502.A2 F453 2024 | DDC 333.79—dc23/eng/20230830
LC record available at https://lccn.loc.gov/2023035077

Cherry Lake Publishing Group would like to acknowledge the work of the Partnership for 21st Century Learning, a Network of Battelle for Kids. Please visit Battelle for Kids online for more information.

Printed in the United States of America

Note from publisher: Websites change regularly, and their future contents are outside of our control. Supervise children when conducting any recommended online searches for extended learning opportunities.

Stephanie Feldstein works at the Center for Biological Diversity. She advocates to protect wildlife and helps people understand how humans impact nature. She lives in the woods in the Pacific Northwest with her rescued dogs and cats. She loves to hike and explore wild places.

CONTENTS

Introduction

Blowing Up Mountaintops

The Appalachian Mountains are one of Earth's oldest mountain ranges. They're rich with **biodiversity**. Bears, bats, and birds live in the mountain forests. Snakes and turtles live there, too. Wildflowers grow there. But in the rocks below the surface are seams of coal. The tops of the mountains are blasted off to get to it.

Mountaintop removal is an extreme form of coal mining. Miners usually go underground to access coal. But with mountaintop removal, the land is destroyed to expose it. The forests are cleared. Then explosives are used to blow up the rock. Hundreds of feet are blasted off the mountains. The trees can't grow back.

The rubble is dumped into the mountain streams. It's filled with toxic heavy metals. It poisons the streams. Fish and salamanders live in those streams.

A Giant Industry

There are eight times as many people on the planet as there were in 1800. That many people use a lot of energy! It takes a huge **industry** to produce all that power.

The United States has less than 5 percent of the world's population. But it uses about 17 percent of the world's energy. Most of it comes from **fossil fuels**. Almost 1 million oil and gas wells are in the United States. The country has more than 2.6 million miles (4.2 million kilometers) of oil and gas pipelines. There are more than 3,400 fossil fuel-fired power plants. About 700,000 miles (1.1 million km) of power lines carry electricity to cities and homes. That's enough power lines to wrap around Earth 28 times.

Energy use continues to grow. But it's not used equally. The wealthier people are, the more energy they use. But more than 1 in 10 people in the world don't have electricity at home. Increasing **renewable energy** can help. Solar panels make it easier to get power to more people.

Crayfish and mussels live there, too. Nearby communities use the streams for drinking water. More than 500 mountaintops have been destroyed for coal. About 2,000 miles (3,219 km) of streams have been ruined.

Energy is a big part of our lives. It keeps us warm and turns on lights. We use it to cook food. Energy powers machines. Every industry depends on it. But the energy industry is wrecking the planet. It's hurting wildlife and humans.

Human industry has changed the face of the planet. More than 8 billion people live on Earth. People are living longer. We're healthier than ever. But everything we use or buy comes at a cost. Human industry uses natural resources that wildlife needs. It creates **pollution** and waste. It can affect human health, too. Our industries put a lot of pressure on nature. The most pressure comes from wealthy countries like the United States.

We need a healthy planet to survive. We need clean air and safe water. We need **ecosystems** with lots of different wildlife. We need a stable climate. We can have energy without fossil fuels. We can power the world with renewable energy that's good for people and the planet.

CHAPTER 1

The History of Energy

Energy has always been part of human life. We used the Sun for heat. We burned wood for warmth and cooking. Ships moved with wind-powered sails. Water mills helped grind grains as early as ancient Greece. Oil and gas were used for light and heat in China more than 2,000 years ago.

Ancient civilizations used steam from water to fire furnaces. They used it to power small machines. Animals such as horses and cattle also powered many machines. But the course of history changed in the 1700s. The modern steam engine was invented. It was powered

Tractors weren't widely used by farmers until the 1930s and 1940s. Before that, they relied on horses and mules for heavy farm labor like plowing fields.

by coal. This new engine was easy to use. It could replace dozens of horses. And it was cheaper than taking care of the animals.

Coal helped fuel the Industrial Revolution. It was dirty and smelly to burn. But growing cities needed more energy. And many nearby forests had already been chopped down. Coal helped people use machines instead of making things by hand. It was the beginning of today's giant industries. Industries from plastic to fast fashion couldn't exist without machines.

Energy and Human Health

Fossil fuel energy creates greenhouse gases. Greenhouse gases trap heat in Earth's atmosphere. This causes climate change. Climate change affects all life on Earth. It causes deadly storms. Insects like ticks and mosquitoes thrive in warmer weather. They expand to new places. They carry diseases.

Drilling, refineries, and power plants poison the air and water. Burning fossil fuels releases toxic pollution into the air. The pollution can make it hard for people to breathe. It can cause heart attacks and strokes. Scientists say fossil fuel pollution causes one in five deaths worldwide.

Energy improves our health in many ways. Furnaces keep us from freezing in winter. Air conditioning saves lives in summer. Hospitals need electricity for medical equipment. Refrigeration keeps medicines cold. It helps keep food safe.

Renewable energy doesn't create air pollution. It can provide the clean energy needed to keep us healthy.

Thomas Edison's Holborn Viaduct power station
operated for only 4 years, from 1882 to 1886.

In-home electricity was initially only available to the wealthy. J.P. Morgan (front right) was the first man to have electricity in his private residence.

In 1882, inventor Thomas Edison opened the first coal-fired power plant. It provided electricity to part of London. Soon, factories were using electricity. It was safer and cleaner than burning coal on site. It made it easier to produce even more goods. Electricity was used in homes, too. It changed the way we live.

Motorized cars were also invented in the 1880s. In the early 1900s, Henry Ford made a car that more people could afford. Cars and cheap gasoline changed the world. People could get around easier. But nature was paved over for highways. Cities sprawled into suburbs.

TROUBLE WITH TRANSPORTATION

Every airplane flight has a big impact on the climate. One long flight can produce more greenhouse gases than some people create in a year. It can be 100 times worse than taking a bus.

Cars and buses can run on electricity. Electric vehicles don't emit greenhouse gases. They can be powered by renewable energy. It's harder to make electric airplanes. But people are working on ways that airplanes can use less fuel. They're working to reduce airline greenhouse gases.

Henry Ford made cars more affordable through his use of the assembly line.

During the energy crisis in the 1970s, many gas stations ran out of gas. Others rationed gasoline.

A man walks past industrial smog-covered homes in Birmingham, Alabama, in 1972. People were realizing they needed to do more to fight climate change.

By the 1970s, people learned that cheap energy came at a price. Countries with lots of oil controlled the global supply. When they cut off that supply, prices skyrocketed. People began to realize fossil fuels polluted the air. They realized **climate change** was threatening life on Earth. A new energy revolution was needed.

CHAPTER 2

The Environmental Cost of Energy

Today, more than 80 percent of energy comes from fossil fuels. Fossil fuels are the biggest cause of climate change.

Climate change causes global warming. Rising temperatures make places too hot to live. The heat makes **drought** worse. Drought happens when there's not enough rain for a long period of time. There's not enough water for plants to grow. There's not enough water for people or animals. Drought makes wildfires more dangerous.

Warmer temperatures also cause extreme storms. That leads to flooding and landslides. Melting glaciers add more water to the oceans. The seawater rises onto islands and beaches.

A forest fire rages through British Columbia, Canada.

Fracking requires powerful hydraulic drilling equipment.
Fracking releases pollution into the ground and air.

Many wild animals nest on beaches. They rely on plants for food. Storms and fires destroy their **habitat**. Climate change could drive more than one-third of all wildlife species to **extinction** by 2050. Climate changes make it harder for people to survive, too.

We've already used the fossil fuels that were easy to access. It's harder to get them out of the ground now. The industry has to drill deeper. It uses **fracking** to get oil and gas. Fracking blasts water, sand, and toxic chemicals deep underground. It breaks apart rocks to release fossil fuels. The chemicals poison water and air. Fracking can even

Changemaker: Rebecca Hernandez

Rebecca Hernandez grew up in the foothills of California's Santa Ana Mountains. She loved the wild plants and animals around her. Now she's a scientist. She studies how the energy industry impacts wildlife.

Huge desert solar farms are harming the environment. They hurt wild animals like desert tortoises. Hernandez researches where we can put solar panels without harming nature. She studies how solar power can help communities.

Hernandez works at the University of California, Davis. She started the Wild Energy Initiative. It brings together experts on energy and nature. They find ways to solve sustainability problems. Hernandez got an award from the Center for Biological Diversity for her work.

Forests can help absorb greenhouse
gases and keep our air clean.

cause earthquakes. The only way to stop climate change is to keep fossil fuels in the ground.

Nuclear energy doesn't create much climate pollution. But it creates dangerous waste. There's no good solution to dispose of it. And nuclear accidents are deadly to people and wildlife.

Renewable energy creates very few greenhouse gases. But it can have other harmful environmental impacts. Giant solar farms take over large stretches of desert. They harm the wild animals and rare flowers that live there. They take over the land on which these animals and flowers live. Wind turbines kill birds and bats. But careful planning can avoid these threats. Renewable energy can be put in places where it won't harm wildlife.

FORESTS FOR FUEL

Using forests for fuel isn't green energy. Burning plants releases greenhouse gases. It releases more gases than burning coal. It creates dirty air pollution. It destroys wildlife habitat.

Cutting down trees for fuel makes climate change worse. That's because healthy forests absorb greenhouse gases. Saving forests is one of the best ways to fight climate change.

Powering Ahead

Scientists say we must reduce greenhouse gases. We need to cut them in half by 2030. It's the only way to avoid the most serious climate impacts.

We don't need fossil fuels for energy. And we don't need to destroy habitat for renewable energy farms. We can produce energy by using structures that already exist. One way is to put more solar panels on rooftops. This doesn't cause additional damage. And it keeps energy close to where it will be used. That means fewer power lines are needed. This is called **distributed energy**.

The National Renewable Energy Laboratory studied where solar panels could go. They believe more than 86 billion square feet (8 million square meters) of U.S. rooftops could hold panels. That could generate about 40 percent

Solar panels can be installed on factory and warehouse rooftops.
Many people have them on their homes.

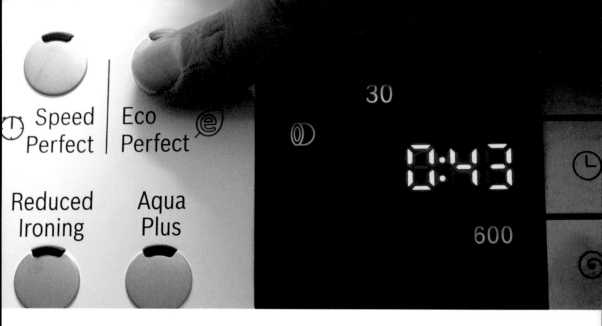

Many home appliances now have an "eco" option available.

We could get even more energy by putting large solar panels on parking lots, over parking spaces. They could provide shade for cars. They could power electric vehicles. They could create energy for nearby buildings. Floating panels could go on water canals. They can be placed in almost any area developed by people.

Energy efficiency is important, too. It means using less energy for the same jobs. Newer appliances are usually more efficient. New washing machines use 25 percent less energy than old ones. Efficiency helps the energy industry have a smaller impact.

Stopping energy waste also helps. Poorly sealed windows leak heating and air conditioning. Devices that suck power even when turned off are called "energy vampires." Some examples include microwaves, hair dryers, and video game consoles. We don't have to produce as much energy if we stop wasting it.

SOLAR SOLUTION

California was the first state to require solar panels on new homes. The panels have to be able to power the homes all year. The policy helps people use fewer fossil fuels. It makes renewable energy more accessible. It makes builders think about energy efficiency.

Other types of new buildings will also have to use solar power. Solar panels will be on new schools and offices. They'll be on new hotels and stores. Cities across the country are passing similar rules.

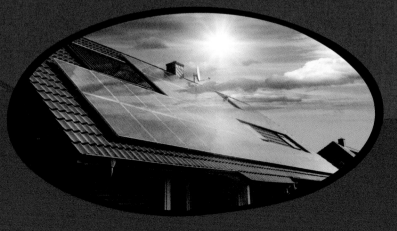

The Future of Energy

Scientists are working to make solar panels more efficient. Scientists have developed thin-film solar panels. They're thin and lightweight. They're flexible. They can be used on lots of different surfaces.

These panels can also be transparent. They can be put on windows. You could still see through them. Solar windows would add a lot of power to buildings.

Thin-film panels don't last as long as other solar panels. But the technology is improving rapidly. Researchers have made panels that are thinner than human hair. They generate 18 times more power than other solar panels. They hope to see them used everywhere.

People are fighting for climate change action. Many people are looking for clean energy alternatives.

We can meet our needs with distributed energy. Electric companies are worried this will make them lose money. And the fossil fuel industry doesn't want to stop production. They try to make it harder for the renewable industry to grow. But communities are fighting for clean energy. And the renewable energy industry is growing faster than any other kind of energy. The future will be powered by

Activity
Build a Solar Oven

Solar power is the energy of the future. But you can harness the power of the Sun without high-tech gear. It takes only a few basic supplies to make a solar oven.

You can use the oven to heat many kinds of food. Try making a mini pizza on an English muffin. Or melt cheese on a tortilla. You can also make s'mores.

Here's what you'll need:

- Cardboard box with an attached lid, like a pizza box
- Box cutter (and an adult to help use it)
- Ruler
- Aluminum foil
- Glue stick
- Duct tape
- Clear plastic wrap
- A stick to prop open the lid

1. Have an adult help you use the box cutter to cut a flap in the top of the box. Use the ruler to measure three sides to make a window. The fourth side should stay attached.

2. Use the glue stick to cover the inside of the box with aluminum foil, including the inside of the window flap.

3. Open the lid of the box. Cover the window you made with two layers of plastic wrap, one inside and one outside. Secure with duct tape.

4. Wait until midday on a sunny day. Close the lid. Use the stick to prop up the flap. Then put your food in a pie tin or glass plate. Place it in the oven. Close the lid, watch your food cook, and enjoy when it's done!

Learn More

Books

Eboch, M. M. *The Future of Energy: From Solar Cells to Flying Wind Farms.* North Mankato, MN: Capstone Press, 2020.

Hirsch, Andy. *Science Comics: Electricity: Energy in Action.* New York, NY: First Second, 2023.

Sneiderman, Joshua, and Erin Twamley. *Everyday Superheroes: Women in Energy Careers.* Minneapolis, MN: Wise Ink Creative Publishing, 2022.

Sneiderman, Joshua, and Erin Twamley. *Renewable Energy: Discover the Fuel of the Future With 20 Projects.* White River Junction, VT: Nomad Press, 2016.

On the Web

With an adult, learn more online with these suggested searches.

"A Guide to Climate Change for Kids" — NASA

"Fossil Fuels Explained to Kids" — Earth.org

"Just for Kids: What's Climate Change?" — Climate Reality Project

Glossary

biodiversity (biye-oh-dih-VUHR-suh-tee) the variety of plants and animals in nature

climate change (KLIYE-muht CHAYNJ) changes in weather, temperatures, and other natural conditions over time

distributed energy (dih-STRIH-byoo-tuhd EH-nuhr-jee) energy produced close to where it will be used

drought (DROWT) a long period of time without rain

ecosystems (EE-koh-sih-stuhmz) places where plants, animals, and the environment rely on each other

energy efficiency (EH-nuhr-jee ih-FIH-shuhn-see) the use of less energy for electricity, heating, and cooling

extinction (ik-STINK-shuhn) when all of one kind of plant or animal die

fossil fuels (FAH-suhl FYOOLZ) fuels like oil, gas, and coal that come from the remains of plants and animals and are burned for energy

fracking (FRAK-ing) process of blasting water, sand, and toxic chemicals deep underground to break apart rocks and release fossil fuels

greenhouse gases (GREEN-hows GAS-ez) gases that trap heat in Earth's atmosphere and cause climate change

habitat (HAB-uh-tat) the natural home of plants and animals

industry (IN-duh-stree) all the companies that make and sell a kind of product or service

pollution (puh-LOO-shuhn) harmful materials released into the environment

refineries (rih-FIYE-nuh-reez) industrial plants that separate fossil fuels into different products like fuel and plastic

renewable energy (rih-NOO-uh-buhl EH-nuhr-jee) energy that comes from sources nature will replace and doesn't pollute air or water

Index